Tolerated to Celebrated

It's All About the Relationship

Ernie Lansford

Maxwell Leadership Certified Coach

Tolerated to Celebrated, It's All About The Relationship

QR Codes within are for quick reference of authors and materials that have influenced Ernie Lansford. **There are NO AFFILIATE LINKS**.

Published in Indian Harbour Beach, FL, by
Business Development Concepts, LLC.
274 Eau Gallie Blvd. Ste 310
Indian Harbour Beach, FL 32937
(770) 595-8616

Business Development Concepts, LLC books, on-site seminars, and Lunch 'N Learns may be purchased or scheduled for educational, business, fundraising, or sales promotional use.

For information, please email ernie@ernielansford.biz

ISBN: 9798286039456

The Parable of the Tolerated Professional Visitor and the Celebrated Customer Success Master™

In the midyear days of a not-so-distant year, a seasoned sales leader—a business development specialist from afar—quietly arrived at the company's gates to lead the global sales team.

Unlike others, he wasn't chasing transactions to hit EBITDA targets. His focus was different: build partnership relationships with the internal team and the company's customers, and EBITDA would soar. And as the weeks passed, he did precisely that.

He reviewed personnel files and conducted one-on-one interviews, not to intimidate, but to gain a deeper understanding that would allow him to add personalized significance to each team member. He asked two simple questions during the meetings: "How can I serve you better?" "If you were me, what would you do in this role?"

He soon recognized that the Pareto Principle was at work within the team. Eighty percent of the revenue was being generated by only 20% of the field representatives. The rest, well-meaning professionals in title, had become little more than tolerated professional visitors in the eyes of their customers.

They confused activity with accomplishment and wore skepticism like a badge of honor.

"This is a brutal economy," they murmured. "The media is right—recession looms, tariffs will destroy us."

And so they gathered. Not in client offices, but in the Inns of Starbucks and Dunkin, doom-scrolling social media, and watching news clips on their phones. They sipped lattes and shared recession forecasts. They didn't discuss strategies, ideas, or customer impact. They compared month-to-date excuses and shook their heads at what they perceived as unrealistic quotas. "*We could achieve more sales than the company can imagine if it would create new products and improve our existing products, create greater brand awareness, thus creating pull-through demand,*" was a common excuse.

Meanwhile, the new sales leader quietly built a new kind of team.

Field representatives who added value and significance. Professionals who understood the power of relationship equity. Among them was a rising star—a rep who didn't just meet expectations; he exceeded them.

He wasn't chasing orders. He was building trust. He was developing partner relationships.

And when the tolerated professional rep visitors heard of his results—of the relationships he developed and the business he generated—they were astonished.

"How is he doing this in this market?" they asked. "Doesn't he know there's a recession coming? "The talk of tariffs is killing business!" Doesn't he realize customers are sitting on bloated inventories? It must be CRM trickery… or luck."

Then one day, as they gathered again at the coffee shop, their thumbs scrolling and spirits slumped, the seasoned sales leader stopped by and pulled up a chair.

They asked him, "Who is this new guy you brought in—during economic headwinds, impending tariffs, and fearful buyers—and yet, he's thriving?"

The sales leader smiled, ordered an iced cold brew coffee, and said, "The one you speak of isn't lucky. He's intentional. He's a business development professional who serves through, vs. sells to. He understands his customer's customer. That's why his clients promote him, beyond vendor status, to partner. He shows up early. He reflects. He prepares. He doesn't pitch products—he creates value with business development and market expansion ideas and concepts. He doesn't chase quotas—he adds significance.

While you mope in faded company T-shirts, sharing gloom and social media articles, complaining about what you think the company should do to help you succeed, he studies to sharpen his leadership and relationship-building skills. He raises the standard by which future sales professionals will be measured.

He speaks with clarity. He never badmouths competitors. He uplifts his clients. And because he adds significance to our profit opportunities, his customers chase him, not the other way around.

At the end of the quarter, while you rehearse alibis, he reviews commissions." The room fell silent. He continued:

"You say it's magic? There's no magic. But he does have four helpers: Positive Attitude. Preparation. Perspiration. Inspiration.

These companions walk with him every day, through objections, gatekeepers, and procurement rounds. He earns trust with truth. He delivers value and significance without discounting our prices or his integrity.

His clients don't call him a sales rep. They call him something else...A *Customer Success Master*™."

And with that, he stood, finished his cold brew coffee, and said:

"Now go out… and do likewise.

INTRODUCTION

Why Relationships Still Matter

Through six decades of experience in sales and leadership, working with regional and global brands, I've discovered a simple truth that often gets lost in the noise: personal and professional growth is fueled by strong relationships. Not transactions. Not pricing structures. Not the latest CRM software or AI tool. Relationships!

In my early years, I was measured by the revenue generated, the number of units I sold, the revenue-to-goal ratio, or the number of new accounts I opened. And for a while, that was enough. But over time, I realized that transactions alone won't build a lasting career or a legacy. What matters is who we serve, how we serve, and what kind of connection we create.

When I stopped chasing transactions and started building meaningful relationships, the transactions chased me. I was promoted from tolerated professional visitor to celebrated partner..

I've shared this principle for decades in boardrooms, with field reps, in team meetings, and in keynote addresses. I call this mindset *Customer Success Mastery™*, built around one foundational truth:

Customer Success is My Path.
Adding Significance to others is My Mission.
Celebrated Relationship is My Goal™.

Relationships aren't static. They grow, shift, and evolve. Or sometimes, they stall. After observing relationships across various sales channels for over 60 years, I've noticed that every client and customer sees salespeople through a lens—a perspective shaped by their experience, expectations, and emotions. That perspective determines how much they value the salesperson and whether they invite them in deeper or keep them at arm's length.

I did not write this book to tell you how to run your business or craft the perfect slide deck. I don't promise that you'll increase sales by X percent. What I do offer is the truth I've earned from a lifetime in the marketplace, building genuine relationships. This book isn't about gimmicks or shortcuts—it's about transformation. It's about moving from being a tolerated presence to a trusted and celebrated partner. It's about becoming the kind of person others want to work with—not because of what you sell, but because of how you show up to serve. I've been all the characters in the parable. In the early years of my career, I was a professional tolerated visitor, simply showing up and hoping for a purchase order.

This book wasn't shaped by psychology studies, focus groups, personality assessments, or high-powered consulting firms. I imagine most analysts at firms like McKinsey or Gartner wouldn't even glance at it. But I didn't write it for them. I wrote it for people like you—sales professionals and relationship builders looking for something deeper. While this book was developed independently, I gratefully acknowledge the leadership insights of John C. Maxwell, whose teachings have shaped many of my personal and professional convictions. Mr. Maxwell is, in my view, the world's leading voice on organizational leadership. What he calls leadership, I call Customer Success Mastery™. Based on nearly 60 years of experience, I've found that most salespeople don't see themselves as organizational leaders, especially without direct reports. That said, every sales professional has the opportunity to lead by the way they serve. That's what this book is about. It's based on what I've learned since 1966—as a retail store clerk, a territory rep, a regional team leader, and eventually, SVP of Sales in the B2B2C channel. At every stage, I've discovered that relationships are everything. And yet, most of us have no framework to understand or improve them. That's why I created the Five Levels of Sales Relationship Pyramid—a simple, powerful model to help you move from being merely tolerated… to truly celebrated

Relationships are everything.

"Our Brand is not what we say it is, but what THEY say it is".
Marty Neuimeier

It's our relationships that define the *THEY* in Mr. Neumeier's Quote.

One dictionary defines a relationship as "how two or more people or entities are connected, or the state of being connected." Yet in our on-demand digital click-and-ship world, relationships are taken for granted, undervalued, or assumed. I believe relationships are more than transactional—they're transformational.

"We attract who we are, not what we want."
James Allen from As A Man Thinketh

Relationships help us to define who we are and what we can become. OUR BRAND, who we are, is grounded in the relationships we build. Most of us can trace our successes to pivotal relationships that helped us develop our brand of who we are..

Midway in my career, I realized that chasing transactions led to burnout. Additionally, I had no desire to create a brand as a transaction chaser or deal maker.

When I stopped chasing transactions and started building deep, meaningful relationships, the transactions chased me. My shift in mindset became a trademarked concept, *Customer Success Mastery™*. My definition of Customer Success Mastery™:

"A Customer Success Master embodies the mindset, desire, commitment, and ability to help customers get to where they want or need to go faster and more efficiently than they would without the help and guidance of a Customer Success Master™

And my definition is built around a straightforward statement or mantra:

Customer Success is My Path. Adding Significance to others is My Purpose.
Celebrated Relationship is My Goal™.

This goes beyond the traditional "Know, Like, Trust' sales model. It's about being valued because we add significance to others, being someone our clients appreciate and celebrate.

"Success is what we do for ourselves; Significance is what we do for others." *John C. Maxwell*

That's how we build relationships. Yes—relationships are everything. But let's be clear: there's no line in a financial direct deposit or online field labeled 'relationship.' Only transactions—dollars and cents—appear on our bank statements. That's why healthy relationships in business must eventually lead to measurable action. Customers want to be invited to engage, not be ignored or treated like a financial wallet. Relationships open the door, but it's the transaction that walks through it. And when the relationship is genuine, deep, and authentic, the transaction becomes more than a sale—it becomes, as Rabbi Daniel Lapin says, a certificate of appreciation. A tangible way a customer says, 'Thank you for the significance you've added to my life or business.'

So yes, build deep, meaningful, authentic relationships and remember to extend an invitation to engage. Build relationships on a foundation of conducting business in a way that exceeds expectations in return—a simple yet effective concept.

I introduce my relationship framework—a simple, visual model I developed working with customers, building partnerships, and adding significance to their journey.

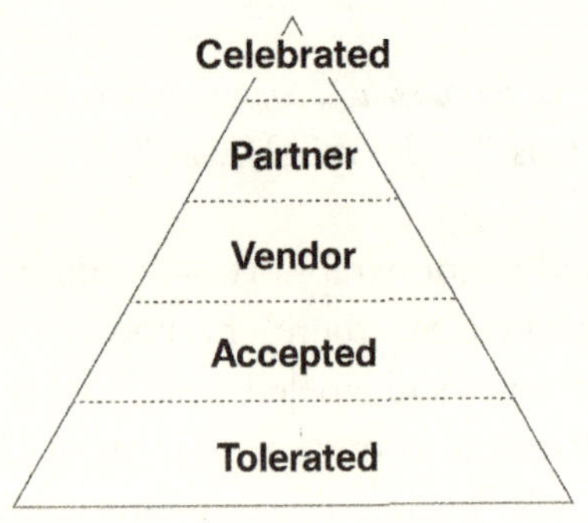

The Relationship Pyramid

Five Levels That Define Your Impact

Tolerated: At the base of the relationship pyramid, we're just a title or a necessity—no trust, no equity, just obligation. Tolerated relationships are shallow, transactional, and fragile—positional, not personal. Customers interacting with salespeople initially confine them to the box of negative first impressions. Their experience with previous salespeople is the cause of this. But there are keys to escape the box of first impressions, and we'll uncover them as we climb the pyramid.

Accepted: Moving to Accepted feels like a shift; they know the salesperson and welcome them. It's not just about recognizing an existence; customers begin to engage. Acceptance is permission-based—the salesperson is planting seeds for deeper relationships through consistency and quality. It's better than Tolerated, but it's not enough. Without engagement, there is a risk that the customer will lose focus. Still, this level matters—it's the first key to unlocking the box of first impressions because relationship-building is working.

Vendor: Vendor is a mile-marker—the customer chooses the salesperson and their company or brand. There is enough trust to say yes, potentially by requesting market insights, not just product or brand information. Vendor status is better than Tolerated or Attention, but it's a delicate relationship because a chosen replacement is easy to implement if a better option becomes available. The Vendor level isn't the goal or destination. The key that unlocked the box of first impressions is nearly forgotten. Vendor relationships are a doorway to deeper connections; vendor status should not be a destination.

Partner: Partnership means shared success. The salesperson is not just delivering—they are making a difference by adding significance. This is where deep business development occurs. Mutual success is co-created. Solutions to problems are provided. Selling is no longer merely an action because serving is at the forefront of awareness.

Celebrated: This is rare air, the pinnacle of all relationships, both personal and professional. Celebrated relationships are rare and sweet. They are earned by showing up, adding significance, and staying consistent. These customers value the salesperson's insight and remain in the relationship for years, even if one's title or company changes.

TOLERATED

Present, But Not Preferred

If you've ever been in a meeting and thought, "They're only listening to me because they have to," you were in the **Tolerated** zone.

At this base level of the relationship pyramid, we're known only by title or necessity. There's no trust, no equity—just obligation.

Back in 1971, I landed what I considered my dream job: territory sales representative with St. Louis Music. What I didn't know at the time was that I was the 11th rep assigned to that region in just eight years.

One store owner looked me straight in the eye and said, "I don't know if I'll ever see you again, but I need Alvarez Guitars, so I have to work with you." That was it. I wasn't Ernie. I was just the next guy. In that moment, I wasn't valued. I was tolerated.

Based solely on his previous experiences, I was boxed in by negative first impressions—trapped by the failures of those who came before me. And I had to learn how to be rightfully released from the box of negative first impressions.

This still happens today.

Think about cable monopolies, solid waste providers, or even the U.S. Postal Service. Many hold their position not because of excellent service, but because of exclusivity. People continue using them, not out of preference, but because they have no better option. They're tolerated.

Here's the strange part: even when a better solution comes along, like a newer, faster, more responsive streaming service or an independent solid waste management provider, customers are slow to embrace it. Why? Because that newcomer is also confined to the box of negative first impressions. They're guilty by association until proven otherwise.

In your world, the same dynamic may play out. You may be required to work with a customer that you perceive as difficult—an entity your leadership selected for reasons outside your control: their online presence, a competitor's implied success, hundreds of 5-star reviews, or a variety of personal assumptions. Perhaps you feel that engaging with a customer at a level higher than your current customers requires greater attention than you think you can provide, or you've heard 'rumors' that their customer service isn't stellar. Regardless of the reasons, it's easy and *comfortable* to place them in the box of negative first impressions. You enter the conversation holding your breath, unsure how it will go. You anticipate friction in pricing, programs, or general business operations. You assume pricing challenges that might compromise your principles. You've taken the worst preconceived ideas and placed them in the box of negative first impressions without going deeper to understand the customer and possibly their customer. Because you put them in the box of implied negative first impressions, they hold the POSITION of customer rather than an authentic relationship. You deem them TOLERATED.

But let's be frank—TOLERATED is bi-directional. Salespeople are tolerated, too. Some customers view salespeople as obstacles to conducting meaningful business. Possibly, there is a perception that salespeople slow things down, complicate workflows, or add too many layers, including commissions, to the process. Whether earned, inherited, or perceived, that perception becomes a barrier. Based on hearsay or past frustrations with salespeople in general, the customer places you in the box of negative first impressions, too.

That box is overcrowded—unfortunately, most of us placed there are innocent. We're living in someone else's story until we prove our own.

Whether you're a manufacturer, sales rep, or client, if you're new, misunderstood, or simply following someone who left a bad impression, you could find yourself stuck in the box of negative first impressions. Tolerated relationships are positional. And positional relationships are almost always temporary. They're shallow. They're transactional. And unless we find a way out of this implied box, the relationship will remain fragile and forgettable. Wondering how to spot when you're just being tolerated? Here's how it shows up.

Signs of a Tolerated Relationship

- Unless necessary, calls are avoided, and voice-mail messages are not returned. E-mails requesting an appointment often require multiple sends before a response is received.
- They say things like, "Just send me the quote."
- You're there but not respected.
- They only meet with you because policy or contracts require it.
- No benefit statements from you explaining the benefits and net gain received by working with you.
- You're left out of early conversations or planning meetings.
  If you're informed after decisions have already been made, it's a sign you're not valued, just necessary to fulfill an order.

- They refer to you by your company name, not your own.
  If you're constantly called "the [Your Company] rep" instead of by name, it often signals they haven't invested in knowing you, and don't intend to. You're a function, not a relationship.

- You're never introduced to others in their organization.
  When customers value the relationship, they open doors. If you never get past your single point of contact, you're stuck in the tolerated tier.

What Keeps You Stuck Here

- Relying too much on your title or the reputation of the product/brand you represent.

- Creating impending event catastrophes to secure a purchase order on your timeline, implying that you need to make quota.

- Often bragging about your activities with other customers.

- Being reactive instead of proactive.

- Listening to defend/reply vs. understanding.

- Talking twice as much as you listen.

- Not following up or not delivering on promises.

- Failing to ask questions that show you care about their goals

- The enforcer mindset: 'These are the rules—take it or leave it

Action Points to Rise Above Tolerated

- Display excellence in all interactions—Again and Again—Consistency builds familiarity. Familiarity builds comfort. Comfort leads to trust.

- Do What You Say You'll Do—Reliability is the first step toward credibility.

- **D**eliver Small, Unexpected Value—Send handwritten notes—request permission to share ideas. Deliver beyond the transaction.

- Ask Better Questions—Move from "What do you need?" to "What are you trying to accomplish?"

- Be Patient, But Intentional—You can't rush trust. But you can earn it—one thoughtful step at a time.

Moving from Tolerated to a higher level requires you to be seen not as a transaction, but as a person with integrity. Someone who shows up, follows up, and stands out. Someone who works diligently to add significance to the customer, rather than chasing transactions to fuel personal success.

ACCEPTED

You're Known, But Not Yet Essential

There's a subtle shift or bridge to the next level. When a relationship moves from Tolerated to Accepted, you feel it. They know your name now. You've been around enough times that they recognize your face, maybe even joke with you about your timing or your donut choice. But let's be clear—this isn't a partnership yet, not even vendor level yet. This is still a cautious, arms-length relationship. You're 'ok', but not relied upon. You're known—but not yet needed. You've earned a small measure of permission, but not deep trust. But that's progress. The box cutter required to open the box of negative first impressions is on the table. And that matters.

What Accepted Means

Moving from Tolerated to Accepted feels personal and relational—The customer welcomes you. It reflects a meaningful internal shift in perspective, where someone sees you not just as an existing entity, but also begins to consider you to be professionally engaging.

I recall when I first felt accepted during my early days as a representative. I wasn't the 11th guy in 8 years anymore. I was "Ernie, the Alvarez Guitar Rep." They didn't necessarily trust me with significant decisions, but they started accepting and acknowledging my presence. They asked about new models. They remembered our last interaction; they smiled when I walked in. Why? Because I did what I said I'd do. If I didn't know the answer, I found it. If I said I'd follow up in 48 hours, I did. And that kind of consistency, especially back in the days of pay phones at the local gas station, snail mail, and handwritten thank-you cards, meant something.

It was the start of them liking me—not deeply, not loyally, but politely. This is a permission-based level. At this level, I was planting seeds for deeper, more meaningful relationships. They connected me with consistency, quality, ease of working together, and other benefits.

From their perspective, I was no longer an interruption, I was no longer just tolerated—I was growing into a perceived value, an option to consider.

I enjoyed the Acceptance level because it was better than Tolerated, but it was still only Level Two of the relationship pyramid. I could not camp here because being accepted without engagement leads to lost opportunities. Please understand—this level mattered. It was the first real sign that relationship-building was working. The box cutter on the table was ready to be used, allowing me to escape the box of negative first impressions.

How did I move from tolerated to acceptance? I showed up after the first visit. I followed through on the commitments I made. I displayed excellence in my actions. I did the small things—like answering questions quickly, sending a thank-you card, or remembering something personal. They didn't dread my arrival anymore. They may even have looked forward to it. But I was still being evaluated.

Signs of an Accepted Relationship

- They remember your name.
- You've had a few quality conversations.
- They're open to your input, but only in certain areas
- They view you as a vendor, not the vendor
- You're on the list—but not yet on the shortlist
- You get invited in, but not pulled in.
- There's polite rapport, but limited commitment.

What Keeps You Stuck Here

- Thinking that being liked is enough. They are my friends, how can they not do business with me?
- Failing to go deeper by asking insightful questions.
- Not understanding their customer's customer.
- Waiting to be invited into the bigger conversation.
- Focusing more on your product than on their process.
- Delivering the minimum instead of finding ways to delight by going the extra mile.

- Avoiding risk—staying in the safe, likable zone.

Action Points to Rise From Accepted Level

- Listen Intentionally — Don't just answer questions—start learning their patterns, pressures, and people. Seek to understand vs reply or respond.

- Show That You Remember — Bring up past conversations. Follow through with details that show you're listening.

- Offer Small Wins — Introduce a tool, a layout, or a process that makes their work easier, not just your product easier to sell.

- Connect the Dots — Help them visualize how what you offer benefits their customer. If you don't know their customer, ask.

- Earn Invitations — Keep showing up, being valuable, and asking how you can support, not just how you can sell.

- Be Responsively Proactive — Anticipate their needs before they ask.

- Be Easy to Work With — Reduce friction. Make them glad they know you.

The ACCEPTED level begins to open the aforementioned box of negative first impressions; it serves as a box cutter to higher levels on the relationships pyramid. If you serve well here, you'll be invited in. Ultimately, the goal is to move beyond being known or liked. You want to be chosen. That's where we're headed next.

VENDOR

You're Chosen, But Still Replaceable

The Vendor level is where business is officially done. At this level, you're not just liked. You're trusted, at least within a defined lane. You've earned a place at the table because you've proven that you deliver, follow through, and make life easier for the customer.

They CHOOSE you. They call you when they need something.
They quote you regularly—or even exclusively in some cases. You may even be referred to others. There's elation and a feeling you've arrived, right? Nope, not yet.

The Trap of the Vendor Level

It's easy to confuse chosen with winning the race. But at the vendor level, you're still vulnerable. You've been selected or chosen, but so has the next vendor. And the next. And the one offering a better deal, faster shipping, a friendlier tone, or more margin.

Vendor relationships can be stable, but they're rarely unshakable.

I've seen talented sales professionals stop here. They think, "I've got the business. Why fix what isn't broken?" And while they're standing still, taking the relationship for granted, someone else is showing up, serving deeper, and creating real value for the customer's customer. And just like that, they're out. Vendor level not anchored in mutual success. It's not rooted in shared values. Vendor trust is fragile. It can be reversed overnight. Vendor status is better than tolerated or accepted. You are officially out of the negative box of first impressions, but the box hasn't been recycled yet. It's in the storage bin in the back, waiting to be used again. It's no longer labeled as 'negative first impressions'; the 'negative first impressions' monikers have been marked through, and it's now just a relationships box, like all the other boxes in the recycle bin. Some of those boxes contain past, unused relationships. Vendor status is not the goal. It's a door to grow deeper, not a destination

How I Knew I'd Become a Vendor

Looking back, I realized I'd been promoted to vendor when customers started asking for things outside of our standard catalog.

They'd say, "Hey Ernie, what do you know about this…?" or "Can you help us source that…?" It was no longer just about price or fulfillment—it was about trust. They valued my insight. They wanted my input. But they still hadn't let me inside their business. I was still standing on the outside, with access to the loading dock, not the boardroom. I was among a group of vendors in an active relationship box along with others, including my competitors. And I had to be careful not to confuse respect for my reliability with respect for the significance I brought to them. One could be replaced. The other couldn't.

Signs of a Vendor Relationship

- They actively choose you for specific needs.
- You're part of their go-to list. Some customers elevate you to preferred status.
- They introduce you to others in their circle, but cautiously.
- You're trusted on a functional level. You're not yet involved in strategy or long-term planning.
- They invite you to submit quotes without bidding wars.
- You receive last-minute "we trust you" orders.
- You're copied on internal emails as a courtesy, not a requirement.
- You get looped in early, but not early enough to influence direction.
- They say things like "You've always been reliable for us."

What Keeps You Stuck Here

- Thinking functional trust is the finish line.
- Leading with product, promotions, and deals instead of purpose.
- Selling to the buyer without understanding the internal and external influencers.
- Focusing on today's PO instead of tomorrow's outcome.
- Failing to serve through your customer to their customer.
- Avoiding conversations about the customer's vision. Vendors rarely ask, "Where are you trying to go?"
- Measuring success only in units shipped or your revenue compared to the same reporting period of the previous year, not outcomes delivered.
- Relying too heavily on the current buyer instead of connecting across the organization.

Action Points to Rise From Vendor Level

- Shift From Transactional to Transformational. Do more than fulfill orders—start solving problems.

- Ask Higher-Level Questions—What's affecting their business long-term? What opportunities are they missing?

- Serve Through, Not Just Sell To—Help your customer succeed by helping their customer thrive. That's where significance starts.

- Build Cross-Functional Trust—Become a bridge between departments. Introduce efficiency, not just products.

- Plant Seeds for Partnership—Say things like, "Have you considered…?" or "What if we tried this together…?"

- Show Up With Insight. Don't just bring pricing—bring perspective. Be a meaningful specific rather than a wandering generality.

- Speak Their Language. Know enough about their peer group to mirror their lingo and priorities.

- Build Horizontal Relationships. Get to know the influencers across departments—finance, operations, marketing, not just procurement.

- Ask How They Measure Success. Then align your service to that.

- Be Ready to Disqualify Yourself. Say, "I'm not the best fit for that, but here's someone I trust." It's memorable and builds integrity-based trust.

At the Vendor level, your customer trusts what you can do.
But at the Partner level, they begin to trust who you are. Your customer is starting to develop a connection with your brand.That's our next stop—and it's where things get both more meaningful and more strategic.

PARTNER

Where Mutual Success Begins

If the vendor level focuses on transactions and reliability, the Partner level is where we begin co-creating value. This is no longer about being "one of the chosen suppliers." It's about being on the radar before they even need something. It's about contributing ideas, not just filling requests. It's about shared goals, mutual wins, and conversations that begin with: "What are you seeing out there?" "What would you do in this situation?" "We'd love your input before we move forward."

At the Partner level, you're trusted not just to deliver, but to think. You're trusted to help shape outcomes. This is rare air in our world. It's also where the relationship pyramid narrows—because not everyone gets here, and not everyone wants to..

Partnership: More Than a Buzzword

This is where things deepen. Partnership means shared success. We're not just delivering a product—we're making a difference, adding significance, making an impact. I became a partner when I stopped acting like a vendor sales representative to my customers. I began training their teams, creating basic planograms to display and sell my products more effectively. I served their business. I stopped asking, "What did you sell?" and started asking, "How can we grow together?"

I wouldn't just present a new model—I'd coach them on how to sell it. That's when I truly began to serve through, rather than sell to. I wanted their store to thrive and prosper. Why? Because I learned a simple truth: If my products were selling out the front door, I didn't have to chase the replenishment purchase order. Replenishment is automatic when success and significance are mutual. That's when I created one of my Customer Success Codes:

"Know your customer's customer. Serve through vs. Sell to."

Let me explain what that meant for me. Remember, my sales channel was B2B2C. My direct customer was the retail music store that sold my products to consumers. Their customers ranged from beginner students to professionals. Those customers also had customers: their audience. Sometimes, that audience (customer) was a parent, siblings, or peers in the family room. It could be a gathering at a coffeehouse, a venue similar to Madison Square Garden, or a house of worship.

My simple point is that our direct customers have customers, too; they're called the audience. My customer's customer (audience) was my indirect customer. When I helped the store salesperson serve their customers more confidently and effectively to please their audience, I added true significance. Not just a sale. Not just a reorder. Significance.

Let's be frank: the word partner is thrown around too casually in business. But in a true partnership, all parties care about each other's success. Risks are taken together. They challenge each other. Everyone is allowed to speak hard truths because the relationship is strong enough to stand it. When I reached this level with my customers, I noticed a significant shift: my customers weren't just buying from me; they were asking for help to grow. Often, this meant answering questions that had nothing to do with a purchase order. That's what partners do—they look beyond the transaction to serve something bigger.

Signs of a Partner-Level Relationship

- You're involved early in discussions, not just during execution.
- You're asked to help solve broader challenges, not just supply solutions.
- They give you frank & truthful feedback—and expect the same from you.
- Your success is tied to their success (and vice versa).

- You speak in we terms—not just you and I.
- You're consulted during major decisions, not after.
- You've helped them avoid a mistake, and they thanked you for it.
- They refer to you as "part of our team" in internal discussions.

Warning Signs That the Partnership Is Taken for Granted

- Failing to provide strategic insight.
- Relying too much on price, perks, or convenience.
- That you no longer need to share the benefits of your products and how your customers profit.
- Waiting to be invited into deeper conversations.
- Not understanding your customer's customer's customer.
- Avoiding difficult conversations or downplaying conflict.
- Believing that the partnership is on an unshakeable footing, and halting marketing expansion and innovation.
- Becoming complacent with being reactive rather than proactive.
- Showing up unannounced without clearly defined customer benefits. Assuming 'they always make time for me, we're partners."

Action Points to Deepen the Partnership

- Understand Their Upstream and Downstream Needs. Who do they answer to? Who do they serve? Serve through that chain.

- Think like a Business Development and Market Expansion Specialist. Bring ideas, not just products. Add perspective, not merely features, advantages, and benefits. Reveal net gains.

- Earn the Right to Speak Freely. Healthy partners don't always agree. But they always have respect. Speak truth with grace.

- Offer Strategic Support. Propose new systems. Suggest efficiency ideas. Help improve their customer experience.

- Practice Serve-Through vs. Sell-To.™ Your job isn't just to close the deal—it's to make them look good to their customer. That's how you earn long-term trust.

- Stay Ahead of the Curve — Share market trends and shifts before they ask.

- Invest in the Relationship — Seek appointments without an agenda to check in because you care, not just because you need something. Send handwritten thank-you cards. Call or text to check in without an agenda.

Partnership is powerful. But it's also fragile. It must be nurtured, not assumed. You can't coast here. You must continue adding significance and insight, not just orders and answers. You must be proactive, present, and persistent in doing the things others simply won't.

Remember the "Relationship box" from the other levels, now in the recycle bin? It's still there. As long as you continue to add more profound significance and your value is recognized, it will most likely not be used again, but it remains in the building. Developing deep, meaningful strategic partnerships is like placing a padlock on the storage bin of the "Relationship box." A true partnership is deep and far more valuable than a mere relationship in a box

And when you do that—consistently, over time—you may just be invited into the highest level of all…

CELEBRATED

Trusted, Remembered, Referred

If Partner is where the relationship gets real, Celebrated is the pinnacle of the relationship pyramid. Celebrated is where it becomes remarkable. This is the level you don't advertise. You don't promote yourself into it. You don't even ask for it. You're invited into it. This is the ADVOCACY Level. The "bail you out" level.

Celebrated relationships are earned slowly, authentically, and often quietly—over time, over years, sometimes decades. It's when clients don't just trust you with the deal. They trust you with their reputation. They endorse you, refer you, defend you, and look for ways to bring you into the room—even when you're not asking.

Celebrated Is Not Common—And That's the Point. You can't have 100 celebrated relationships. You don't have the capacity.
Neither do they. Celebrated isn't scalable—it's selective. And that's the way it should be.

You celebrate a handful of people in your life—maybe your spouse, your kids, a mentor, a lifelong friend. And in business, it's no different. It's not about quantity or bandwidth—it's about depth.

I pivoted out of corporate in 2016 to pursue writing, coaching, speaking, and business consulting. In my last corporate assignment, there were 1,300 accounts in the system. Of the 1,300, 275 provided 80% of the revenue, but 12 were core. Working with my field rep partners, I served these twelve. Two became celebrated. We still call on birthdays. We stayed connected after my role changed. We will pick up the phone at 2 a.m. if we need each other.

Frankly, the Celebrated level is indeed rare air. Achieving a goal for a celebrated relationship is a quest regardless of our current level. These relationships didn't just know me as "the guy who used to sell that brand." They know me as Ernie—a trusted voice, a guide, a friend. Remember my mantra:

Customer Success is My Path. Adding Significance to others is My Purpose.
Celebrated Relationship is My Goal™.

Signs of a Celebrated Relationship

- They mention your name when you're not in the room —and it's always positive.

- They refer you to others even when you don't ask.

- They defend your value inside and outside the marketplace.

- You share mutual loyalty, mutual care, and mutual trust.
- They see you as part of their legacy, not just their latest project.
- You are acknowledged as a key component of their brand, one that has been built over many years.

What Keeps Most People From Ever Reaching This Level

- Chasing volume instead of depth.
- Moving too fast to build a real connection.
- Thinking celebrated means "famous" or "popular."
- Confusing frequent contact with meaningful impact.
- Failing to serve with significance.

Action Points to Sustain Celebrated Relationships

- Show Up Long After the Deal Is Done. Celebrated relationships outlive the contract. Stay in touch. Stay interested. Stay human.

- Give Without a Hidden Agenda. Share something helpful. Make a meaningful connection. Ask how they're doing—without a sales pitch.

- Be a Steward of Their Reputation. Honor them in public and private. Speak well of them. Protect their interests. That's how trust deepens.

- Be Willing to Bail Them Out. Figuratively—and maybe even literally. A celebrated relationship is one where you'd pick up if they called at 2 a.m..

- Don't Overuse the Word.
  Just because you admire someone doesn't mean you've reached this level. Keep this category sacred. That's what makes it special.

One Final Truth About Celebrated Relationships

You can't force them. But you can work to create the conditions for them. You can increase the level of significance you bring to the relationship. Follow through better. Stay longer. Care more. And when you do that enough times, over enough years, for the right people, they'll let you know:

"We're not just doing business with you. We're building something with you."

We've uncovered a fact that not all business relationships are equal. Some are transactional. Others are transitional. A few—very few—become transformational. Those are the celebrated relationships. But here's the good news: You don't need to be born with charisma, own a corner office, or carry a gold-plated title to earn trust, build influence, or create a celebrated relationship. You need to decide. Decide to lead with purpose. Decide to listen deeper. Decide to serve through, rather than sell to. Decide to add significance to someone else's day, business, or legacy. That's celebrated. That's legacy-level. That's brand-building level. And while the celebrated pinnacle may only happen a handful of times in your life, it's worth everything it took to get there. I encourage you to adopt a mindset of a goal to achieve and work toward celebrated relationships with everyone you encounter.

What This Means for You

Let's review our climb up the pyramid.

Celebrated — ADVOCACY

Partner — Inner Circle—Mutual success

Vendor — CHOSEN.

Accepted — PERMISSION.

Tolerated—POSITION.

The bottom three levels can be monotonous—sometimes dreary, even unprofitable. But the top two? They're worth the climb because that's where fulfillment lives. But here's the key: We cannot promote ourselves up the pyramid. Only the customer can promote us to a higher level. That said, they can demote us to. All that we can control is the significance of our input in the relationship.

"The market for adding significance to others is infinite."

I believe people are hungry for more than products, services, or empty promises—they search for alignment, meaning, and trust. The marketplace is filled with voices, noise, metrics, and personalities. The real question we should ask is: What do we believe in? And just as importantly, what do our customers—and their customers

—believe in? Do we believe in adding significance to others by serving through rather than selling to? Do we view customers as ATMs without making deposits?

"You're a pretty good sales rep, except for the nine times you called me 'wallet' instead of 'Walter'."

If our most profound belief is tethered to transactional achievement alone, we risk building temporary value on a foundation of ego. However, if our faith is rooted in serving others with humility and excellence, we begin to operate under a different set of key performance indicators (KPIs). Rather than a Key Performance Indicator, we create a Key Partner Indicator. This is where influence multiplies. This is where our brand is built.

Customer Success Masters™ don't just measure revenue. They measure the ripple effects of the relationships they build. They serve their customers' customers—and sometimes their customers' customers' customers. They stay visible long after the transaction disappears.

Let's be clear: Not everyone is ready for the climb from Tolerated to Celebrated. But the ones who are—those rare few—understand that:

Customer Success is My Path.
Adding Significance to others is My Purpose.
Celebrated Relationship is My Goal™

They don't use that as a slogan. They live it as a standard. Truett Cathy, founder of Chick-fil-A, once said that he would like to be remembered as someone who kept his priorities in the proper order. He used to say (paraphrased):

"We live in a changing world, but we need to be reminded that the important things have not changed, building relationships with our customers."

So, let's strive not just to be chosen…But to be remembered. Not just to be present…But to be celebrated.

"Capital goes where it is welcome and stays where it is well treated."
Walter Writeson, former chairman at Citibank

Deep, meaningful, genuine relationships are like capital; treat them with care and respect.

The Difference Between a Tolerated Professional Sales Rep and a Relationship Builder

- One chases transactions—the other seeds transformation.
- One waits for direction—the other brings insight, energy, and perspective.
- One protects their territory—the other expands their influence.
- One sells to be heard—the other listens to serve.
- One sticks to the script—the other adapts to the story in front of them.
- One checks the boxes—the other creates meaningful breakthroughs.
- One seeks credit—the other shares the win.

Final Thought

Too often, we make bold demands of others—expecting excellence, trust, loyalty, and performance—without holding ourselves to those same standards. We want world-class clients, all-star team members, and high-performing partners. But let's be real: We can't expect to sit at a world-class table if we're not bringing anything of value or significance to it.

In business relationships, value and significance have to be mutual. It's not just about what we're hoping to get—it's also about what we're prepared to give.

We all carry a mental list of what we expect from others. But before we pull out that list, let's ask ourselves: If someone made a list like this… would I check every box on it? As Marshall Goldsmith once said, *"What got you here won't get you there."* It's a sobering reminder that the mindset and skills that helped us achieve early success might not be enough to sustain us at the next level. Growth means letting go of what used to work and developing into someone new

If not, then it's time to stop focusing on what you expect —and start working on who you're becoming. Remember James Allen's quote in the introduction:

"We attract who we are, not what we want."
James Allen from As A Man Thinketh

Growth doesn't happen by hoping for better relationships—it happens by building yourself into someone who earns better relationships. Because the truth is: You can't expect loyalty if you've shown no consistency. You can't expect excellence if you deliver mediocrity.

You can't expect to be celebrated when you're not yet prepared to serve.

Austrian philosopher Ludwig Wittgenstein once described a concept now known as Wittgenstein's Ladder. He wrote that the philosophical tools he laid out were useful only to help the reader climb to a new level of understanding, at which point the reader would recognize that the tools themselves could be discarded. The same is true here. Hopefully, you've identified the level—or box—others may have placed you in. Ideally, if you've climbed, grown, and reflected through the lower three levels of the pyramid, you're now ready to go higher. If my simple pyramid framework has helped elevate your thinking, your mission, or your purpose, then I have fulfilled my goal. I hope that it has helped you recognize the significance of the Partnership level, anchored in the mindset of Celebrated Relationship. At that point, Wittgenstein's metaphorical ladder can be left behind because partnership is no longer a level. It's a way of life.

If you've made it this far, I'd like to say something simple but deeply heartfelt: Thank you for caring about relationships. Thank you for choosing purpose over pressure. And thank you for doing the work that creates a legacy, not just revenue. Because when all is said and done:

Customer Success is My Path. Adding Significance to others is My Purpose.
Celebrated Relationship is My Goal™

And that's a mission worth showing up for—every single day.

R.E.L.A.T.I.O.N.S.H.I.P.S.

I love acrostics. I created this one

R – Respect begins at the first interaction

E – Empathy builds trust

L – Listening is your superpower

A – Authenticity earns attention

T – Time invested creates transformation

I – Integrity is the unshakable foundation

O – Ownership turns mistakes into momentum

N – Nurture long after the sale

S – Significance adds weight to every touch

H – Humility keeps you grounded

I – Influence comes from value, not volume

P – Purpose drives every conversation

S – Servanthood is the way to the top

I do not write to attain bestseller status. My prayer, hope, and desire is that my books inspire the reader to take action and look at the person in the mirror, asking: "Am I adding significance or chasing transactions?" I hope this book has guided you through each level of my experience-based relationship pyramid—what it looks like, why people get stuck there, and most importantly, how to move forward.

Whether in sales, consulting, business development, customer service, or leadership, I hope my pyramid framework helps you understand your current position and how to advance tomorrow.

Ernie's Influential References

The Greatest Salesman In The World By Og Mandino Copyright 1968 by Og Mandino published by Bantam Books by arrangement with Frederick Fall, Inc

Start with Why by Simon Sinek, copyright 2009 by Simon Sinek, published by Penguin Press.

The Power of Significance by John C. Maxwell Copyright 2017 by John C. Maxwell published by Hachette Book Group, Inc.

Success for Dummies by Zig Ziglar, copyright 1998 by IDG Books Worldwide.

How to Be Like Coach Wooden by Pat Williams. Copyright 2006. Published by Health Communications, Deerfield Beach, FL.

Cartoon on page 51 used by permission: Glasbergen Cartoon Service. Fee paid for use.

The 12 Week Year by Brian Moran, copyrighted in 2013 by Brian F. Moran & Michael Lennington, was published by John Wiley & Sons, Inc.

The Poetics of Sales by Ernie Lansford copyright 2018 by Ernie Lansford Published by Business Development Concepts, LLC, Indian Harbour Beach, FL.

Roger Staubach's public speeches.

Effective Selling Through Psychology by Buzzotta-Lefton-Sherberg. Psychological Associates copyrighted it in 1982, and Ballinger Publishing Company in Cambridge, MA.

15 Laws of Growth by John C. Maxwell Copyright by John C. Maxwell 2012. Published by Center Street, Hatchett Book Group, New York, NY

Learning to Lead by Fred Smith Copyright © 1986 by Christianity Today, Inc. A Leadership/WORD Book. Co-published by Christianity Today, Inc. and Word, Inc. Distributed by Word Books (out of print)

Breakfast with Fred Newsletter. Writings from the archives of Fred Smith, former CEO of Christianity Today Magazine, and other companies during his life. Fred was the coach and mentor to many of today's leadership authors.

The Power of Who Copyright © 2009 by Bob Beaudine Published by Center Street for Hachette Book Group 237 Park Avenue, NYC, NY 10017

The Success System That Never Fails by W. Clement Stone ©1962 By Prentice-Hall, Inc. Englewood Cliffs, NJ

The Five Levels of Leadership ©2011 by John C. Maxwell Published by Center Street for Hachette Book Group 237 Park Avenue, NYC, NY 10017

The Business Secrets of the Trappist Monks: One CEO's Quest for Meaning and Authenticity. Copyright © 2013 August Turak. Published by Columbia University Press

Jeff Brown's Read To Lead Podcast

Maxwell Leadership Podcast

Craig Groschel's Leadership Podcast

Ernie's Amazon Author Page

Ernie's Gumroad E-Book Page

Ernie Lansford, a 60-year veteran of the musical instrument and pro audio industry—encompassing Alvarez, Ampeg, Peavey, Mackie, and EAW—has extensive experience in senior leadership roles. In addition to this book, he authored 'The Poetics of Sales' in 2018 and published Marketplace Proverbs Volumes 1 and 2 and Customer Success Codes Volume 2 in 2024, with nine more volumes of Marketplace Proverbs planned. Drawing from years of daily Proverbs readings, his 30-day devotionals provide actionable marketplace wisdom inspired by the Bible as the ultimate business manual.

Ernie plans to travel in a restored 1977 GMC Eleganza Motorhome, hosting Lunch 'n Learns at businesses in exchange for an honorarium that includes books and reflects music industry traditions. He draws inspiration from Proverbs 27:17, "As iron sharpens iron, so one person sharpens another," to fuel his mission of influencing the USA marketplace for God.

Connect with ernie@ernielansford.biz

(770) 595-8616

Made in the USA
Las Vegas, NV
04 June 2025